The *Spirit* of a SUPERHERO

The *Spirit* of a SUPERHERO

SELENE ANTONINI

WESTBOW
PRESS®
A DIVISION OF THOMAS NELSON
& ZONDERVAN

WestBow Press books may be ordered through booksellers or by contacting:

WestBow Press
A Division of Thomas Nelson & Zondervan
1663 Liberty Drive
Bloomington, IN 47403
www.westbowpress.com
1 (866) 928-1240

Scripture taken from the HOLY BIBLE: EASY-TO-READ VERSION © 2014 by Bible League International. Used by permission.

ISBN: 978-1-9736-1477-7 (sc)
ISBN: 978-1-9736-1476-0 (e)

Library of Congress Control Number: 2018900490

Print information available on the last page.

WestBow Press rev. date: 1/16/2018

To *you* and anyone who feels something
inside but just can't explain it.

Author's Note

This book is a collection of my thoughts and more than a few supernatural nudges (that I cannot explain) that have encouraged me to think about the "what ifs" in life. This started as an inspirational book for my grandchildren that included my own real-life experiences that provided an opportunity for me to think about helping them to believe, grow, and discover who they are. Instead it turned into a journey for me to share with everyone—one that God would not let me give up.

Contents

Acknowledgments

I would like to thank my children, Robert, Mitchell, Heather, and Cameron, for giving me their trust and belief that all things are good and happen for a reason. Also, thanks to my grandchildren, Mikayla, Aubrey, Emily, and Maverick, for keeping my spirit young and charged with energy.

Also, I would like to acknowledge family members, friends, and acquaintances who helped forge the experiences and moments that crossed my life and formed me into the person I am today. Without you, I would not have the courage, insights, and gratitude to share this with the world. I have learned so much and am eternally grateful for the time you had to touch my life.

Lastly, I would like to thank the Life Church for sharing the YouVersion Bible app to help me stay focused by providing many devotional insights to ensure I am aligned with my heart and the Word of God.

Introduction

Have you ever wanted to be a real superhero? Have you ever just wanted one special gift that nobody else had? Some special ability that comes from within you that makes people feel good and inspired? No matter where they come from, all people have hidden desires to do great things like helping, protecting, or guiding others. There's a common element in all the superheroes today: they all strive for a better outcome given the circumstances. No matter whether they come from a wealthy background, come from poverty, have a disfiguring disease, or have something different about them (which may make them weird or unusual to people), they are all striving toward the same thing.

> ❧ Superheroes have the ability to help, protect, and feel good about themselves, knowing they made a positive difference in someone's life.

One day I found myself at an airport. I was heading to Texas for work, just daydreaming and watching people around me. I saw many people of all different types and cultures, from newborn babies being held by their mothers to elderly people in wheelchairs being pushed by airport security. I was particularly drawn to a girl about twelve years old; she was "protecting" her mom from the man-eating escalator that was dragging everything under the floor with its steel teeth. She was holding her mom back with both arms extended as if she was giving her life instead of her mother's to the insatiable man-eating escalator. I thought about the drive and dedication we have to protect and guard the ones we love when they are in danger. As I looked closer, I noticed that there was a Captain America shield on her shirt, and it perfectly fit the role she played, which displayed confidence and passion to protect others.

A few minutes later another man caught my eye; he was in his early sixties, and he was looking up at the airport monitors hanging from the ceiling to check on his flight. He had such focus. He was standing very tall and stoicly; his shoulders were perfectly squared, his back was straight, his chest was out, and his hands were squared on his hips. He was staring up like a mighty oak tree that can't be moved. All of a sudden, a boy who was about seven years old, who was running and not watching where he was going, bumped right into him and bounced off, hitting the floor like a tennis ball. The man was surprised because he hadn't seen the boy coming, but he was compassionate, and he turned to help the young boy up and make sure he was okay. As I looked closer at the man, I noticed he was also wearing a Captain America shield on his shirt—how weird is that?

I boarded my plane heading to Texas, and after a while I finally got to my hotel room. It was late, so I opened *USA Today* to pass some time and see what was going on in the business world. I was totally shocked to see Captain America's picture with the title "The Battle Is On for 'America's Superhero' Bragging Rights." It was an article about how the world is not a fun place, and having a hero who is a symbol for good is strangely comforting for a lot of people of all ages. Weird—again. Then, over the next few months, I began to see so many people supporting different superheroes with T-shirts, movies, book bags, hats, and tattoos. Superheroes were everywhere! We have superhero mania. All ages across the world are acknowledging the goodness in so many different superheroes; people need to know there is an ultimate source of goodness out there, and they are just begging to be part of it—and everyone wants in!

So, what gives us confidence to be something great like a superhero today? Is it the actual superpowers, the cool suits, or the fact that everyone loves a superhero and wants to be one? Face it. If you're a superhero, then you're the honored guest everywhere you go. You have to feel good about that! I believe our confidence is driven by a strong feeling of doing the right thing and helping others in the process. All superheroes do the same thing even though they have different abilities—they protect, promote peace, and accept all people as they are.

> ∂ What if I told you that I know the secret
> to being a real superhero—and that I
> want to share that knowledge with you?

Have you ever left a movie with a superhero attitude and become that superhero in your mind? You feel so good and powerful, as if there is nothing but 100 percent pure goodness inside you. You are an invincible force of power that will fight against any bullies. You will stand for what's right, and you will be honest without any judgment by anyone around you. Have you ever felt a tug inside you because you want to do something great in the midst of all the craziness and chaos in the world?

So how do you get there? The same way all superheroes do, silly!

> ∂ Find that driving force inside of
> you, and once that's aligned with
> the right goals, you *will* become a
> superhero to everyone around you.

Sounds so easy, right? But where does that goodness and power come from? And what are the right goals? Believe it or not, it's a real Spirit we have access to, and each of us has his or her own spirit. But often we don't listen to or focus on it, so we are not able to tap into that special power available to us. We're busy comparing ourselves to other people, trying to get the best of everything, and trying to gain more money, be smarter, be more popular, and be more successful based on everyone else's standards in this world—usually measured by how many likes we have on our Facebook page or something like that. But, if we can try to listen to and believe what our spirits are saying, then we may be able to be part of our own superhero story!

> ⤳ You can have an influence on the lives of other people and live your very own superhero story that people will talk about for a lifetime.

Now, superheroes are not perfect, but they strive to make the world around them perfect to live in. Every superhero today comes from a broken family or a bad circumstance, but think about it—something somewhere gave them the confidence, strength, and passion they needed to put all that aside and be what they were meant to be—a positive influence driven by a strong spirit.

It takes some people a whole lifetime to find their spirit, and some never find it. But what if that spirit is out there?

What if something's waiting to help guide the potential and strength you have, but you never asked about it?

What if you can always access that power to keep you strong no matter what happens to you in life?

What if you can make the biggest difference in this world for the ultimate good?

What if I told you that your potential has been inside you all along, and all you have to do is believe in yourself to connect with it?

☙ Imagine the possibilities!

Chapter 1
THE GREATEST ANCIENT POWER

So where does this power come from? Where is the source of all this goodness and personal striving to be someone who leaves a positive legacy behind?

> ❧ Where the ultimate power
> resides is not a secret.

It is the greatest ancient power of all time and in the entire universe, and we've heard about it since the start of humankind. Unfortunately, it's been hidden behind judgment, rules, and laws that people have established throughout history. People today feel they need to belong to something in order to believe in something, and I'm here to tell you that is the furthest thing from the truth. The power *is* within you. The source of this power is not taught to you, and there is no college degree you need in order to understand it. The source of this power is given to you from the one who created you, and all you need is the awareness that it exists for you to use. So just believe, and you will start to feel it come alive.

> ✎ You have the ability to tap into the greatest ancient power of all time and in the entire universe.

The ultimate power comes from the Father who gave us an opportunity to know and experience his Son, Jesus Christ. We have a guide to this strength and power, which is explained in the Bible and in the works of Jesus Christ, so let's look at some history of this awesome ultimate power.

Jesus was a small boy who grew up like all of us in a world full of judgment and anger. It was a world full of disease and sickness and everyday struggles, and the kind of world where people never knew whether they were doing the right thing. He was not born rich, and he didn't want to live like royalty—but he figured life out early in his younger years, and by age twelve he tapped into the highest form of what we call the supernatural today. It's known as the greatest ancient power of the Holy Spirit.

He was able to think clearly and make the right decisions because he had such faith in what he knew—what he believed with all his heart. He was not distracted by things happening around him; neither did he allow himself to be taken up in the drama and emotions of people's lives. He had real superpowers of the Holy Spirit that turned water into wine at a wedding (John 2:3–11), and he was able to feed five thousand people from five loaves of bread and two fish to show his **compassion** for people suffering from hunger (Matthew 14:14–21).

He was strong enough to defeat real demons, and they were very afraid of the ancient power. These were the same evil demons that come to destroy our happiness, forcing us to live in complete misery and making us think we're incapable of getting ahead, loving, knowing what peace is, or being happy. Jesus helped a young boy be free of a demon on his journey in this world, and he encourages us to believe in that same faith (Matthew 17:14–21). Jesus was fearless with his Holy Spirit when he got close enough to the demons. He placed his hand on their heads and used his superpower of the Holy Spirit to defeat the demons, and they never came back (Matthew 8:16). He showed us **protection**, trusting his Holy Spirit to lead him on his way.

He was focused and passionate about helping people. The miracles he performed helped people believe in something good. He wanted to promote goodness and happiness for others so much that he had the power to bring people back to life—a superhero ability I have never seen today. He brought a young girl and his good friend Lazarus back after they died (Matthew 9:18–26; John 11:1–4, 38–44). But he didn't do it to show how great his power was; he did it to ease the pain of Lazarus's sisters and the girl's family members and to motivate them to also tap into the ancient power of the Spirit to spread love and help to others. He showed us **goodness** and made a positive difference in peoples' lives with his Spirit to continue his journey and legacy.

Jesus walked everywhere, and he never complained about not getting somewhere fast.

❧ He knew timing is everything.

Jesus didn't fly like Superman, get into the Batmobile, or run like Flash to get somewhere in record time to "save someone," but as he walked, he had so many other opportunities to do good things for people. Think of all those people who would never get to actually see him or be blessed by his miracles if he had always been rushing ahead for the next "good deed." Peter would have never seen Jesus walk on water (Matthew 14:22–23), or Jesus would never have healed blind people on the side of the road (Matthew 9:27–31, 20:29–34) as he traveled. Think about it! Those people would never actually feel the power and believe if he had blinked his eyes in order to travel through time.

Depending on where our minds are, it's easy to be tempted and fooled. Every day we are tempted to lie, cheat, and deceive just so we look good. And we are tempted to judge those around us, which only makes us feel that we are better. We are trying so hard to be the best and outdo others to show our so-called *power*. But whether or not *we* can be tempted or fooled depends on how strong our spirit is and how we're tuned into it. It's important for us to really stop and think our innermost thoughts guided by our own spirit to ensure we are on the right track. Jesus had his mentor (teacher), the Father—his Spirit—to talk to. The Spirit helped sort out decisions when Jesus was alone on his walks.

Jesus was tempted himself when He was walking alone in the wilderness (Matthew 4:1–2). Now, if we think about the wilderness, we usually understand that it refers to an area of danger where there are a *lot* of things to distract our minds and keep us from focusing. Possibly dangerous animals and unfamiliar sounds might allow our imaginations to run wild and introduce fear into our heads. Then the ultimate test for Jesus came when evil itself spoke to him and tried to steal his powers (Matthew 4:3–11). But Jesus, with his superpower in the form of a shield, stood firm and had no fear or distractions. He confronted evil and told it to go away, speaking with the Father's words. Evil had no chance and knew it, and so it left quietly. Notice Jesus didn't hurt, kill, or banish it to somewhere else in the Universe, but Jesus has compassion and knows his Spirit is always protecting him. He showed us to be **patient** and **peaceful** in any situation.

No matter where we are or how old we are, or what we've done in life so far, understand that we have access to this power of the Father. His power will defend us and reverse anything we have done. The key is that we must believe that we come from something more powerful than anyone can understand in this world.

If you want to start harnessing this power, we need to learn more about when the Spirit found _us._

> ぞ You can't believe in miracles and strength if you don't look for it.

Warning: the ancient power is so great and so vast it's impossible for a single human person to do any of the following:

- feel so much goodness and never understand anger
- trust with so much honesty to be 100 percent transparent and not be hurt
- Give 100 percent unconditional love to everyone without controlling his or her own human emotions

This is some serious power that we have access to, and it's so great that no one other than Jesus had any success in harnessing its true power. The good news is that we have the Father to hold all the greatness of this strength and power for us, and he wants to share.

> ぞ The Father gave you a small piece of power when you started your journey as a newborn.

See John 14:16–17 and 26–27 for more information.

Chapter 2

THE BIRTH OF A SUPERHERO

As we began our journey and started to be formed in our mother's wombs, we were given an opportunity to live. We all have a special personality along with gifts and talents. Some of us may never discover these gifts we were given throughout our lifetime out of fear of insecurity, while others do find them later in life. A few people embrace these gifts and are doing wonderful things to share goodness with their spirits power, but even fewer people are able to use their spirit to guide their superhero abilities the way Jesus did. Everyone living on this planet has the opportunity to tap into the greatest power that ever existed to help people and make this world a better place, but we must stay focused.

✿ How did you get the gift?

Before we were born, we were secure in a world of total darkness. The warm comfort and tight quarters felt like a constant hug that never ended as we kicked and turned in our mothers' bellies. We were always safe in that small confined area we called home. We were familiar with the sound of the voices we heard around us, and they were comforting. Nothing could harm us, and no judgment or expectations were ever put on us. We were relaxed and completely content with the sound of a rhythmic heart beating a minimum of 23,328,000 times as we waited. Our emotions became sharpened as we responded to accelerated heartbeats as we felt excitement or sorrow from our mothers' inner workings. Still not knowing what was going to happen to us, we had no thought because we were in a state of mere existence. That was our first gift from heaven: *total security, comfort, and unconditional love.*

As each one of us came into this world on that special day, we struggled to find our way into an environment of unknowns. We have the opportunity to be something, be someone people will remember, make a positive impact on others, live our story. As we took our first breath in this world, a funny thing happened. We didn't come alone. A spirit followed us. This was our second gift from heaven: *a friend who holds all the ancient power available and who will be with us forever.*

Some may think a spirit is something we have to conjure up in a séance or only interact with in magical realms. What if the spirit is just another extension of you—your identical twin in a special superhero story called your life?

A spirit was given to each and every one of us, and each spirit is unique here on earth, as each person is unique. Your spirit is part of you, but the difference is that the spirit does no wrong. It never lies, is completely honest, loves unconditionally, and always protects and guides you. What a cool concept! You have your very own superhero—with superpowers!

> ๖ You were given a spirit to help make you right. You can use it to make this world right.

As children growing up we watched and learned, and then knew what to do based on the behavior and beliefs of the people around us. Our parents guided us. But there is something else that is *deep inside of us*. Some of us are more in tune with our spirits when we are born, and we maintain that strong connection as we get older. It gives us a strong moral character and a healthy positive outlook on everything. Others are led down a different path where they are persuaded or tempted to more attractive opportunities despite their spirit-led character. No matter what path we go down, we all have the spirit ready and waiting for the day we want to leverage that power again.

> ๖ Your first step is to find it within you so that you can tap into it.

Chapter 3
YOUR SPIRIT

❧ As a child, you were guided and protected
by your spirit. It watched over you as you
slept and nudged you in the right direction.

As a kid, I was usually quiet, but that didn't mean I didn't care about people around me. I knew some people who had strong opinions about stuff and wanted everyone to see things their way. I also knew some people who seemed outright obnoxious and rude. But no one really asked for my opinion because I was quiet. I learned early to keep my opinions to myself. Otherwise, I knew I had better be ready to "fight to win"—not in a physical sense, but either verbally or mentally. Neither tough love nor fight or flight applied to my character.

❧ Don't mistake my kindness for weakness.

What makes us feel that way? If we grow up with all that around us from the time we were small, why do we feel awkward or out of place when we're in certain situations? Sometimes we back ourselves into corners when we don't wish to be seen. At other times we may have to present our opinions and justify why we feel the way we do. What if our spirits are nudging us and reminding us that we are not on the path we were chosen to walk?

As kids, we have to build our confidence in what we do because we are always looking over our shoulders for approval. We don't really know what we feel, so we just act out or go through the motions. But we do know and feel when something is just not right. Some call it a gut feeling; others call it intuition or signs that seem to be around us. Whatever we call it, it's our spirit reaching out to catch our attention.

> ❧ Coincidences are the spirit's greatest
> tool for capturing our attention.

As adults, we see emotions fly all around us. We learn to cope with situations by watching how other people deal with things. We have more confidence in what we know than we did as children, but we have been taught how to respond based on life experiences. Some people become angry, depressed, and confused with conflict. Others become focused and dominant. They drive solutions down people's throats, forcing a win situation for them as others cower. Very few will sit back and see both sides without judgment. They will be patient and wait until the answer reveals itself through our spirits. Emotions are fickle and ever changing. This is why it's dangerous to do things based on high emotions without giving consideration to everything involved. Our spirits will guide us in the right direction. *We must think before we act!*

Every day our spirits speak to us in a way no one can comprehend. Sometimes it's through music, a book, a TV program, something a friend says to us. It's always something that just resonates and stays with us all day. Or it could be nagging signs that we see throughout our week related to something we feel that is heavy on our hearts. Communication from the Spirit is a gift, and it's a special gift if we listen. It fuels us with the passion and truth about what drives us to be good and set examples for those around us. God uses the Holy Spirit as a bridge to us, helping with the communication we don't know how to express. God's thoughts are far greater than ours. Some may say it's a language we can't understand, but he's given us the Spirit to always be available and help when needed. The good thing is that the Spirit doesn't allow us to give up. It constantly nudges us in the right direction so we can choose to stop and listen.

When we have the power of the Spirit living in us, we can speak words of wisdom and truth to help others in need. We know what's right and can take action to make things right. We will stand firm and strong, ready to defend and protect at all times, never tiring. We can counter any pressure or negativity with kindness and patience. We are selected to be part of God's warriors, and as we tap into our own spirits, we become superheroes on earth. We know how we should live to help others, but what keeps us strong and focused all the time?

> ❧ He helped you by giving you a superhero suit of your very own.

Chapter 4
THE SUPERHERO SUIT

Our spirits gives us access to a superhero suit that contains six critical pieces we can wear until we are spiritually mature enough to live like a superhero every day without thinking. This helps us develop the skills we need to be strong and listen to our inner spirit to make a positive difference in somebody's life; in other words, to be a great superhero. Our suits are recorded in history as the Armor of God (Ephesians 6:10–13) and contains the following items:

- a belt
- a breastplate
- shoes
- a helmet
- a shield
- a sword

Each item has a special purpose and power, and all together, the suit is a source of ultimate power against all evil.

> ↪ Superheroes must know what powers their suits have in order to use them correctly.

Let's look at what each piece does.

The Belt of Truth

A belt is not only meant to hold up your pants. It's also the foundation for the rest of the suit, providing strength and stability. If we didn't have belts to keep our cores stable, we would end up getting injured when we overexerted ourselves. Even weightlifters wear belts to keep them strong and aligned when they are lifting a tremendous amount of weight. But there's a magical power in the Belt of Truth as well; it helps us tell the difference between the truth and trash. The truth is Spirit-driven truth, and if we wear it properly, we will have the knowledge to know truth from trash so that we can make the right decisions and always be truthful (Ephesians 6:12).

The Breastplate of Righteousness

A breastplate covers the entire chest, and this piece protects our hearts. If we lived by our hearts and not our heads, we would be forever happy and love unconditionally. If we didn't have our breastplates in place, our hearts would fill up with other feelings like fear, rejection, shame, jealousy, and anger, all of which keep happiness away. Righteousness is truth in action. A single lie from someone affects what we think, and if our hearts are not protected, we start to believe that lie in our hearts, giving us wrong impressions and forcing us to judge others unfairly. The Breastplate of Righteousness not only protects our hearts, it also helps us take heartfelt action and make good daily decisions (Ephesians 6:14, 4:25–26).

The Shoes of Peace

When you're playing tug of war, how important is it to wear the right shoes? Without a good solid shoe that holds to the ground, we slip and fall, knocking down everyone around us. Peace is a superhero element that the shoes must have. Peace helps us remain calm and not be distracted. When we wear the Shoes of Peace, no matter what chaos is around us, we will be able to stand firm and be ready for anything that comes our way (Ephesians 6:15; John 14:27).

The Helmet of Salvation

Most superheroes wear some sort of head covering. Spiderman and Captain America wear soft head coverings, but Batman and Iron Man wear hard helmets. We have the Helmet of Salvation available for us. Our helmet protects us from voices, thoughts, and lies we hear in our minds. Those things distract us when we want to take action, and they usually prevent us from taking action. How many times have you wanted to do something but didn't because of the thoughts in your head? Thoughts direct our actions, and we want to stay focused so that we can do the right thing and make good choices (Proverbs 4:23). Wearing our helmet provides constant focus and guarantees our salvation in heaven (Ephesians 6:17; 2 Corinthians 10:3–5; Hebrews 4:12).

The Shield of Faith

The Shield of Faith helps guard us from any other distractions before they hit us. When we see trouble or self-doubt coming, we lift our shields, and they not only deflect what was intended to hurt us, but each time our shields are hit, we are energized with faith and courage so that we can take action and do something and not stand in fear. It's not just any shield; it protects and charges our spirits with more faith and courage to show us ways to follow through on our actions. Our shields recharge us every time they are hit, so use yours with determination (Ephesians 6:17; 2 Corinthians 10:3–5; Hebrews 4:12).

The Sword of the Spirit

The sword belongs to the Spirit, and by wearing the superhero suit, we have the authority to summon its presence whenever or wherever we need it. The sword is double edged and sharp enough to slice through rocks and mountains with a single stroke. It contains all of God's words etched in its blade. God's Word is an ultimate weapon that, when used properly, will always triumph for *compassion, protection, goodness, patience* and *peace* as our history has shown us. So be sure to sharpen it by learning more everyday about his Word and plans for our superhero adventure (Ephesians 6:17; 2 Corinthians 10:3—5; Hebrews 4:12).

The belt, breastplate, shoes, and helmet are all things we wear. The shield and sword are tools we use to stop distractions and help us focus. We need to wear *all* the armor, not just certain pieces, as a superhero. What would Batman do without his utility belt or Captain America without his shield? To be in perfect condition, we need to use all the pieces together to achieve spiritual greatness as the best superhero ever!

      ↬ Create your world. Don't
      let the world create you.

Chapter 5

YOUR SUPERHERO ADVENTURE

☞ Whatever you focus on you become.

Every superhero gets his or her greatness from something—Iron Man from the power of an element, Spiderman from the bite of a laboratory spider, Hulk from engineered gamma rays, Captain America from human intervention and an ultimate source of greatness. They all have great weapons but what do they all have in common after their bizarre transformations? They are driven by pure goodness and righteousness! They all share dedication, a true reflection of honesty, and the desire to help or protect those less fortunate in this world by tapping into their given power and sharing it to promote peace.

We were all given a spirit that gives us access to the ultimate ancient power. No matter what your background is, where you currently are in life, or what you're doing today, there is always an opportunity *now* to be the superhero you were meant to be. You can be free from your own thoughts or misconceptions and the effect on our life, and you can be free from the way others perceive you. This world drives our behaviors, and people drive our actions so that we can be accepted. The Spirit is real, and it tries to move us in the right direction. But whether you are able to hear depends on your capability to listen to the power that is around you. We must use our superpower to hear when everything around us is screaming for different directions. If, for a moment, you just feel your spirit, you may be able to tap inside to the greatest ancient power of all time and make the biggest difference.

☙ How will you respond?

Do you focus on positive things?

Do you live *in* the moment or *for* the moment?

Do you *let* things happen or willfully *make* things happen?

Do you listen to others more than you "tell" or share?

We make a lot of choices every day, from what to wear first thing in the morning to how we respond to other people throughout the day. We have a lot of responsibility to make the right choices, and sometimes with great responsibilities come the feeling of control or personal success in what we've done to make us feel better. A strong human desire tugs at us to feel that we've controlled the situation or succeeded in what we set out to do and seized the day! But we must be careful that it doesn't drive our actions.

Our world puts a lot of emphasis on control and personal success, so much that everyone strives for it to show his or her power and strength compared to that of other people. In reality, there is no measure of success because everyone sees success differently. For some, success is crossing the finish line in first place; for others, it's just finishing the race no matter how they place. Some people gauge success by actually running in the race whether they finish or not, and maybe for some, just struggling with commitments and signing up was their success! People have goals, not success; we determine our own level of success.

> ☞ To succeed or fail is not the
> goal, but just doing will help you
> grow stronger as a superhero.

When we take a step to do something, right away we assess the situation. We wonder *if* we are capable or not because we analyze *if* we will most likely succeed or fail before we even start. We allow that succeed-or-fail judgment to control our every move.

The only thing success or failure tells us is that either we are great at something, which is usually easy, and we keep going, or there are obstacles stopping us, and it's too hard. Nobody fails easily. If we do then we didn't overcome the obstacles. We simply chose to give up. Don't think of the outcome. Just step and let your spirit lay down the path you're meant to take.

> ↷ The power of control is only in providing motivation to help through union.

We don't have the power to actually control situations, but we have the ability to lead, making the right choices for a good outcome when others are involved. When people feel they are in control of the entire situation, they do not give credit to everyone involved, and they usually have a selfish motive to prove to others that they have power.

For example, when Captain America gave directions on how to lead people to safety in New York, he was not in control, but he had a plan that he shared. It was the police captain who heard him and liked his plan. The captain was able to guide people to safety with the help of his team. Multiple people joined together to help a solution. That is an example of a controlled plan, not a controlling person, that helped the situation.

ↄ You are not controlled by
people; rather, you are controlled
by fear of following your spirit.

Think about how you can be the best superhero ever. Let your spirit help you. Equip yourself with your superhero suit and focus on your ability to help, protect, and feel good about yourself, knowing you can make a positive difference in someone's life.

Our spirits don't allow us to give up. It constantly pushes and puts ideas into our heads, and if we only listen and follow through, we will see and feel the future that was meant for us. We will be able to help other people, provided our values are aligned with *our spirits*.

Chapter 6
CONCLUSION

How are you aligned? Is it time to change and step up to what the Spirit has for you? Are you opening yourself up to possibilities and potential without any constraints? Decide today to take a step and be courageous. Be ready to lead the next generation into life because you *are* driven by your spirit.

I challenge you to continue this book by writing your own story. Share it with everyone. You can choose to impact the lives of others by encouraging them to believe in themselves, leveraging the beauty and power of the Holy Spirit.

☞ Not everyone is a story teller,
but everyone has a story to tell.

Ask for the courage and begin today a journal of your inspiration to help align the world again as a real Superhero, and if you need a push to motivate you, check out these verses: 2 Timothy 1:6–7; Isaiah 41:10; Psalm 118:6, 27:1; and Romans 8:31–32.

Readers' Guide

Introduction

- How many instances of superhero references do you see around you in a day? In a week?
- How do you think people feel about superheroes? What makes them want to support and promote a superhero?
- What circumstances or limits do you have in your life and in your mind that prevent you from being a superhero today?

The Greatest Ancient Power

- What are some ways that Jesus showed his superpowers?
- What are some ways he chose not to show his superpowers?
- What did he show us about using superpowers?

The Birth of a Superhero

- Imagine what your superhero twin is like.
- What are his or her strong superpowers? What common elements do you share?
- What are some examples of instances when you felt there was something else there helping you?

Your Spirit

- How can you stay connected with your spirit?
- Does your gut feeling align with your spirit's superpowers?
- How many coincidences have you simply ignored and treated as "weird"?

The Superhero Suit

- Which piece of the suit do you feel is your strongest part and how do you use it?
- Which piece of the suit do you need to work on in order to make it stronger?
- How can you remember the pieces of your suit all the time?
- How often do you wear the whole suit?

Your Superhero Adventure

- Do you ask for your spirit's guidance and help every day in different situations?
- How can you help your spirit?
- What can you do to make a positive impact on people around you?

Challenge: Build your Superhero Story

Think about the future—the next day, week, month, and year—and how you would play a superhero, leveraging your spirit to guide you. List the things you would do to make a positive impact on specific people and the directions in your life.

Create a small story of your "next week" and try a few of your ideas. Share your story with everyone to show your superhero spirit!

References (Index):

YouVersion app
Holy Bible: Easy-to-Read Version (ERV)
English
© 1978, 1987, 2012 Bible League International

Printed in the United States
By Bookmasters